Prayer from a Magdalena Jail Cell

poems by

Abby Templeton-Green

Finishing Line Press
Georgetown, Kentucky

Prayer from a Magdalena Jail Cell

Copyright © 2017 by Abby Templeton-Green
ISBN 978-1-63534-359-5 First Edition
All rights reserved under International and Pan-American Copyright Conventions.
No part of this book may be reproduced in any manner whatsoever without written permission from the publisher, except in the case of brief quotations embodied in critical articles and reviews.

ACKNOWLEDGMENTS

The following works have been previously published in Sixfold 2012, and were a winner in the Sixfold 2012 poetry contest:

The Moment Before
2009 Subaru
Highway 15
What is Left
Aftermath

Publisher: Leah Maines

Editor: Christen Kincaid

Cover Art: *The Letter*, original artwork by Diego Rodriguez-Warner

Author Photo: Nache Greene

Cover Design: Elizabeth Maines McCleavy

Printed in the USA on acid-free paper.
Order online: www.finishinglinepress.com
also available on amazon.com

Author inquiries and mail orders:
Finishing Line Press
P. O. Box 1626
Georgetown, Kentucky 40324
U. S. A.

Table of Contents

During

The Moment Before 1

Prayer from a Magdalena Jail Cell 2

2009 Subaru Legacy 4

Highway 15 5

Before

Frontotemporal Dimentia (FTD) 9

Stages 10

Photo of the Two Dans 13

That Morning 15

After

The Coroner Wants Me to be Sure 19

To Make that Sound Stop 21

Aftermath 23

What Is Left 24

*For Daniel
& the whole La Manga Tribe*

*"Come now, come from where
you have stayed in the earth."*

—Tzotzil prayer to call the soul

During

The Moment Before

On the inside of the windshield
he saw their reflections
and the blur of a coyote
on the horizon.

He knew then
that time slows down
when you are airborne
as if you are about to throw
your first punch,
or lean in to kiss a girl.

Underneath the sound
of crunching were sixty
years of song, a hundred
prayers made of cloud and dirt.

He wondered about saguaro cactuses
would they grow through upholstery,
would planted shards of glass
grow taller than a Durango Ficus,
would his daughter come to this spot,
place a cross on the side of the freeway
and scratch his name
into earth?

Prayer from a Magdalena Jail Cell
Legislación Local, Artículo 389:
Mexican law proclaims any highway death to be manslaughter

His face is my face
though he does not wake.
Driven this stretch a hundred times
now it feels like dream.
Now I am stuck with these damaged hands,
with this hundred time road.

Carcass of dog stuck to pavement road
where vultures know us by face.
This road like a hand
tugging, like God forcing us to wake.
He used to dream
of desert, of a time

with no going back. That was the time
when life was not severed by road,
when nightmares were not dreams
and time was not the face
of a clock with its constant reminder to wake
and pluck windshield from hands.

I remember his hands
braiding her hair before this time.
When I wake
I am road,
when I sleep it is his face
I see: making clouds appear, dreaming.

I remember when dreams
were made up of hands
caressing, when faces
were made of moon and song, when time
did not stop for road
and the three of us woke

early and three of us slept sound. There is no waking
from this dream
of road
where desert hands
reach through a horizon of time
to take more than the reminder of a face,

as if to say: do not wake him even with hands
of mountain and dirt. At times you will dream
he is road, at times the quiet face of desert night.

2009 Subaru Legacy

I was equipped for journey, although I did not mean to fly
or end up inside out, a shell of my own purpose.
I am sorry for the twisting
that I caused, for the pavement I could not reach.

Now I know more than the veins on a map.
I know the ditches that accompany freeways.
I know the meaning of these freckled roads
adorned with wooden crosses and Virgin Marys.

I never was a shield.
I am a mass of metal.
I saved all I could that day.

Highway 15

I have always known blood. From Niño de Guzman to the steady chase of foyuca, heroin and marijuana. I am crammed with trucks, decorated with potholes, a black top scar that runs for 1,432 miles. When they speak of me they tell you what I'm not: undivided, unlighted, lacking shoulder. Without me it would all be bramble and naked desert hills. I connect Hermosillo to Guaymas, La Frontera to D.F. I am a prayer of convenience, un gracias, a whip of speed. I could tell you that I am cursed: shadowed by the Tropic of Cancer, littered with swollen dreams, haunted by promises of the undelivered. I toss and crumble. I shriek and slither. When the cars stack up I am silent, just a wail of wind on greedy, teethy track.

Before

Frontotemporal Dimentia (FTD)

He hadn't always been sick,
there was a time, before,
when he could still remember
my favorite drink,
what type of gas to put in the truck,
Paco, our cat.

The doctors had different names for it:
Frontotemporal Disorder,
Frontal Lobe Degeneration, Pick's Disease.
I just knew it was moving
fast, exceeding
the prescribed timeline.

I remember the extended family camping trip
when we played the newlywed game.
No one knew why
he was getting all the answers wrong.
When did you first meet Maggie?
What song did you dance to at your wedding?

That same vacation,
we took the hike through Copper Canyon,
the desert brush scraping our calves,
fridgit birds and vultures eyeing us from above.

That was when he said it,
that he'd rather
just keep walking,
abandon himself
to the cracked earth of desert,
than to go back
to pretending
not
to have forgotten.

Stages

I.

Goddamn it.
                The birthday party—
could've happened to anyone.
I know my kid's school for god's sake,
just can't remember the block.
It's been years
and the neighborhood is changing.

II.

Later, I remember all the answers:

    -Ladies Night at the Flying Bull Lounge
    -Stevie Wonder, "Isn't She Lovely"

I remember her
waiting
like the rest of them, she wanted to believe
that the moments
were inside me, if not swimming around in my head,
at least they might have burrowed a small nest in my heart,
dislocated, but present,
like the tattoo I got that summer,
just can't remember why.

III.

~~Paco~~
~~Cat~~
~~Pet~~
House   Animal

It's the words.
The words are the problem.
~~I can't find the words.~~ They're in my head.

Like a ~~library~~
                                    book

store

but all the books are

                        ~~checked out~~

  ~~out of stock~~

                                                gone.

IV.

The paper signs
around the house
are written in different colors:

Feed me!
Turn me off!
Lock the door!

        I wander
                          around
            the house:
                                  an engine
left

            on.

V.

I dream of a time
           with no time,
                      with no helpful
reminders
or

mishaps.

I am   ~~overcome with~~
                                the desire

to submerge
               into ~~streams~~
                       ~~rivers~~
                            water
to
    fall
            forward
                                into desert

to do what needs doing.

Photo of the Two Dans

He never should have survived the first crash,
the crash of '65.
That's what his mother said
showing me the photo of the two Dans:
friends born a week apart
and a block away from each other.

The photo was taken right before
they flipped the 1954 Volkswagon van
five times off Durango river bank.

Somehow they made it out: firemen plucked them
from mangled metal and the sinking of river.

The Dans with their wavy hair and tinted glasses.
In the background is the yellow van
with its white top and Navajo curtains hanging.
Behind that is the burlap of asphalt,
native plants and trees.

There should be a photo of his mother
her hands clasped,
tracing the sign of the cross over her chest.
And one of his father:
circling the vehicle, assessing the damage,
finding it easier to quantify the geography
of windshield and tire burn
than to look his son in the eye,
than to admit to believing in miracles,
to the goddamn magic of being alive,
to thanking one dandelion root
and river rock for moving
or not moving
just so.

*   *   *

I guess that's why she didn't cry out
when she got the call from Magdalena:
life on borrowed time
is a rubber band
pulled too tight.

That Morning

We were the first to leave the beach,
to pack up sleeping bags, and faded tent.

He said he was tired, ready to get out
of those clothes, take a hot shower.

It was early morning, no wind.
The dogs didn't bark.

He ate granola and yogurt,
sipped hot water with ginger root,
left the spoon on a rock
and put his shoes on before his socks.

I heard the clicking of time in my ear,
my finger a tracking device
tracing and charting the roads on the map:
250 miles to Nogales,
another 60 to Tucson.

I got mad at him for forgetting,
for stumbling around with the bag of dog food,
and not knowing what to do with it.

Maybe that was when death slithered into the backseat—
cutting in with cold hands and heavy breath,
looking over my shoulder while I drove,
knowing which moves would be the right ones
and which the wrong.

I wrap myself so tightly around that morning,
praying that one of us will sneeze
or blink too long, take a slow sip of water
and it will somehow change the course.

But nothing changes,
not even in my dreams.

Our car rolled seven times that day,
the desert sun cascading
through windshield's broken ribcage.

After

The Coroner Wants Me to Be Sure

You, of bristled beard,
nose like a bell,
a man who cleared his
throat before he spoke,
made time
for collecting rocks
and counting bats
against city skyline.

You, who stepped ferociously
into the unknown,
who watched
clouds change and howled
with the radio, ate
apples down to the stem.

There is a dent in your forehead
where car crumbled
on top of you. There is a patch
of scalp missing where
we tried to scoop your brains
back in. There is a highway
of gravel ironed into your skin.

The coroner wants me to be sure
that the hands on the steel table
are the same ones
that kneaded dough last December,
that caught a golden trout in Fallen Lake.
The same hands that guided
us through 28 years of marriage,
laced our daughter's shoelaces,
cupped water to drink,
and pushed hair
back behind ears.

The coroner wants me to be sure.
How can I be
sure of anything

        anymore?

To Make That Sound Stop

They will bring you
peach cobbler with homemade crust,
chocolate covered almonds (his favorite),
vegetable lasagna,
red wine,
sleeping pills, even.
Cards with flowers on them,
flowers with cards in them,
photos,
fruit baskets.

They will give you
lockets,
a bicycle pump,
a stuffed bear holding a heart.
Books on death and dying,
books on loss and trauma,
books to write in,
to stack and place
a vodka tonic on top of.

They will offer you
condolences, a shoulder to cry,
invitations to *stop by anytime.*
They will take you on a walk,
put a baby in your arms,
hug you so tight you fall slightly,
giving in, if only for a second.

They will leave you
with a new sense of stillness,
with a guilt that burrows itself in
and stays for the night.
They will leave you
with the items that fill the space
when silhouettes and footsteps   don't.

They will tell you
it must have been
the alignment,
the brake pedals,
they will try to explain

what no one can.

They will not tell you
that they understand—
you both know they don't.
They never flew off Highway 15,
never tumbled in mid-air like a barrel.
They never landed, just as abrupt.

The road came up from under me
snatched me from the driver's seat.
It wanted more than the cadence of rubber,
more than the slow pulse of time travel.

Thud.
Thud.
Thud.

The snapping of white posts marking the shoulder:
anything to make that sound stop.

Aftermath

When the jar of pasta sauce
hit linoleum floor,
it reminded her of windshield
with its splintered hands
ripping through skin.
When the blood of tomatoes
flashed across her cupboards,
it reminded her of earth,
of desert floor reaching inside
what was meant to be out.
She wiped up pulp
with a bathroom towel.
There were stones left
in between her teeth
asking:
where
to put
this mess?
She felt bits of glass twisting
in her left hand like a key
in a door that does not open.
The scar looked like a lifeline
of too many children. A phone rang.
She wondered if there was any reason
to fill air with verbs where there was only
room for scrap metal.
"Do words penetrate wind?"
She would ask if she knew no one would respond,
if she was positive that time moved backward
and that she could cook a simple
pasta dish without freeways
slicing through her kitchen,
without this howling at her feet.

What Is Left

We search for it—
the place in the earth
where you left.

Always, I watch for it,
just after mile marker 48,
before the signs for Magdalena.
Never—
find it.

Always,
 I search the earth for you,
scratch the soil for one last hint.
Never—
find it.
Never find
your shoe
or guitar string.
Never find your black cap
or front tooth,
just red clay
in my fingernails.

How could there be no monument to such tragedy?
How could the desert not erect some statue or totume
warning of the fierce possibilities of life?

Still, the land remains:

bramble and bush continue,
a rusty can sinks further under the surface,
sunrays claw and stretch at this land with the sleeves cut off,
this land that is a rumbling of trumpets,
and you
the angel of prayer
and dirt.

Additional Acknowldegments

I would like to give a special thank you to Joy, Muriel, Justine, Clarissa and Kruch for giving me your love and support in writing about this traumatic event. These words only attempt to make sense of such a tragedy. I hope you can find comfort and a bit of healing in them.

I want to thank the entire La Manga family. Together we laugh, love, build fires, and bake bread; just as we cry, throw dirt on coffins, throw ashes into the ocean and sing until our songs reach the stars.

This book has been a long time coming. As we all know, it takes time, love, words, art and time again, to heal. Remember, it is both memory and imagination that makes the poem.

Abby is a writer and teacher from Denver, Colorado. She is the wife to an art educator and mother to two passionate young children. She received her bachelor's degree from Gettysburg College in Latin American Studies and Spanish and an MFA from Antioch University Los Angeles. She is excited to be part of the Finishing Line Press family. When not writing Abby loves to dance, play soccer and swim.

Her other work includes various publications in such journals as *McSweeneys, Calyx, RATTLE, Pilgrimage, The Mom Egg Review* and a chapbook, *An Avocado Slowly Falling* published by Dancing Girl Press. Abby was the recipient of the 2011 Lighthouse Writers Seven Deadly Sins Writing Contest, the 2012 Sixfold Writers contest prize for poetry and a finalist in the Blast Furnace Chapbook competition. She was also nominated to read at City Council as part of the Imagine 2020 city wide plan.

You can visit her at
fromtheblowtorch.wixsite.com/abbytempleton-greene

www.ingramcontent.com/pod-product-compliance
Lightning Source LLC
LaVergne TN
LVHW041513070426
835507LV00012B/1533